TOP 10
BASKETBALL
SHOT-BLOCKERS

Jeff C. Young

SPORTS
TOP 10

Enslow Publishers, Inc.

40 Industrial Road	PO Box 38
Box 398	Aldershot
Berkeley Heights, NJ 07922	Hants GU12 6BP
USA	UK

http://www.enslow.com

Dedication

For my sisters, Laurinda Lou and Stephanie Sue.

Library of Congress Cataloging-in-Publication Data

Young, Jeff C., 1948–
      Top 10 basketball shot-blockers / Jeff C. Young
          p. cm. — (Sports top 10)
      Includes bibliographical references (p. 46) and index.
      Summary: Profiles the lives and careers of ten of the best shot-blockers in
professional basketball history, including Kareem Abdul-Jabbar, Patrick
Ewing, and David Robinson.
      ISBN 0-7660-1275-1
      1. Basketball players—United States—Biography—Juvenile literature.
2. Basketball players—Rating of—United States—Juvenile literature.
3. Basketball—Defense—United States—Juvenile literature. [1. Basketball
players.] I. Title. II. Title: Top ten basketball shot-blockers. III. Series.
GV884.A1Y68   2000
796.323'092273—dc21
  [B]   99-13636
                                                  CIP
                                                      AC

Printed in the United States of America

10 9 8 7 6 5 4 3 2 1

To Our Readers:
All Internet addresses in this book were active and appropriate when we
went to press. Any comments or suggestions can be sent by e-mail to
Comments@enslow.com or to the address on the back cover.

Illustration Credits: Andrew D. Bernstein/NBA Photos, pp. 7, 9, 10, 42, 45;
Bill Baptist/NBA Photos, p. 25; Don Grayston/NBA Photos, p. 21; Fernando
Medina/NBA Photos, pp. 34, 37, 41; Gregg Forwerck/NBA Photos, p. 17;
Jerry Wachter/NBA Photos, p. 13; John Soohoo/NBA Photos, p. 19; Layne
Murdoch/NBA Photos, p. 14; Nathaniel S. Butler/NBA Photos, p. 22; NBA
Photo Library/NBA Photos, pp. 26, 29; Ron Hoskins/NBA Photos, p. 39;
Scott Cunningham/NBA Photos, pp. 30, 33.

Cover Illustration: Scott Cunningham/NBA Photos.

Cover Description: Dikembe Mutombo of the Atlanta Hawks.

Interior Design: Richard Stalzer.

CONTENTS

INTRODUCTION

IT'S ALWAYS EXCITING AND FUN to make a shot, but it's just as exciting to play good defense and make an opponent miss a shot. A good shot-blocker takes the player he's guarding out of his game, and a great shot-blocker takes the team that he's playing against out of its game plan.

In 1891, James Naismith, who invented basketball, wrote the first thirteen rules of the game. His second rule shows that he expected that shots would be blocked: "The ball may be batted in either direction with one or both hands."[1]

Eighty-two years later, the NBA recognized the importance of blocked shots by counting them as an official league statistic. Los Angeles Lakers center Elmore Smith was the first player to lead the NBA in blocked shots. Smith explained the importance of blocking shots by saying, "You can push and shove underneath. But is there a better way to protect the basket than to stop the ball before it gets there?"[2]

A shot-blocker uplifts his teammates and discourages his opponents by stopping, tipping, and altering shots. A shot-blocker can also create fast breaks by tipping the ball to a teammate.

Height and jumping ability help a lot in blocking shots, but those things alone won't make you a shot-blocker. The best shot-blockers also combine timing, instinct, agility, and the intelligence to anticipate shots.

When I narrowed my list to ten players, I felt like a coach who had to cut a talented player from his team. One way I got the list down to ten was by excluding players whose careers ended before 1973. That left out (perhaps unfairly) great shot-blockers like Bill Russell, George

Mikan, and Wilt Chamberlain. They all played before the league kept track of blocked shots.

I also considered the number of career blocks, average blocks per game, and seasons leading the league in blocks. Awards such as MVP and Rookie of the Year and selection to the NBA All-Star and All-Defensive teams were also considered. You may not agree with all of my selections, but I think they are the ten best.

Here are their stories. Read about them. Learn from them and imitate them. But win or lose, play hard and have fun on the court just as they do.

CAREER STATISTICS

Player	Years	GP	REB	AST	STL	BLK	PTS	BPG
KAREEM ABDUL-JABBAR*	1969–1989	1,560	17,440	5,660	1,160	3,189	38,387	2.6*
MANUTE BOL	1985–1994	619	2,635	171	126	2,077	1,584	3.4
SHAWN BRADLEY	1993–	396	3,124	366	274	1,330	4,338	3.4
MARK EATON	1982–1993	875	6,939	840	368	3,064	5,216	3.5
PATRICK EWING	1985–	977	10,155	2,030	1,025	2,674	22,736	2.7
GEORGE JOHNSON*	1972–1986	904	5,887	929	456	2,082	4,369	2.5*
DIKEMBE MUTOMBO	1991–	603	7,282	900	322	2,174	7,762	3.6
HAKEEM OLAJUWON	1984–	1,075	12,676	2,859	1,977	3,582	25,367	3.3
DAVID ROBINSON	1989–	685	7,881	2,028	1,073	2,323	16,715	3.4
TREE ROLLINS	1977–1995	1,156	6,750	660	512	2,542	6,249	2.2

*The NBA did not keep record of blocked shots until the 1973–1974 season. The blocks per game averages for these players include games played only after the start of that season.
All statistics are through the 1998–99 season.

YEARS=Years played
GP=Total games played
REB=Rebounds
AST=Assists

STL=Steals
BLK=Blocked shots
PTS=Total points scored
BPG=Blocked shots per game

KAREEM ABDUL-JABBAR

IF THEY HAD COUNTED blocked shots when Kareem Abdul-Jabbar began playing in the NBA, the legendary center would probably have at least 1,000 more to add to his career total of 3,189. During Abdul-Jabbar's first four seasons in the NBA, blocked shots were not an official statistic. In the first four seasons that blocks were counted, Abdul-Jabbar blocked 1,094 shots.

Kareem Abdul-Jabbar did many things well in his pro career. It's easy to overlook the fact that he led the NBA in blocked shots for four of the first seven years that blocks were counted as an official league statistic. When you win the MVP 6 times, play on 6 NBA championship teams, and make the All-NBA first or second team 15 times, it becomes easy for people to take those shot-blocking skills for granted. Abdul-Jabbar was so good, he could make blocking shots look easy.

"He always looked like he was playing to music," said Abdul-Jabbar's teammate Magic Johnson.[1]

When Kareem Abdul-Jabbar entered the NBA after leading UCLA to three straight NCAA titles, blocking shots didn't come easily. His defense suffered because he got so many goaltending calls. "I got psyched by the officials early on blocking shots," Abdul-Jabbar admitted. "I got a lot of calls for goaltending and I got to the point for a while where I wouldn't even try to block a shot."[2]

As he became more experienced, Abdul-Jabbar learned when to go for the blocked shot. For nine consecutive seasons (1974–82), Abdul-Jabbar was among the top three shot-blockers in the NBA. During those nine seasons,

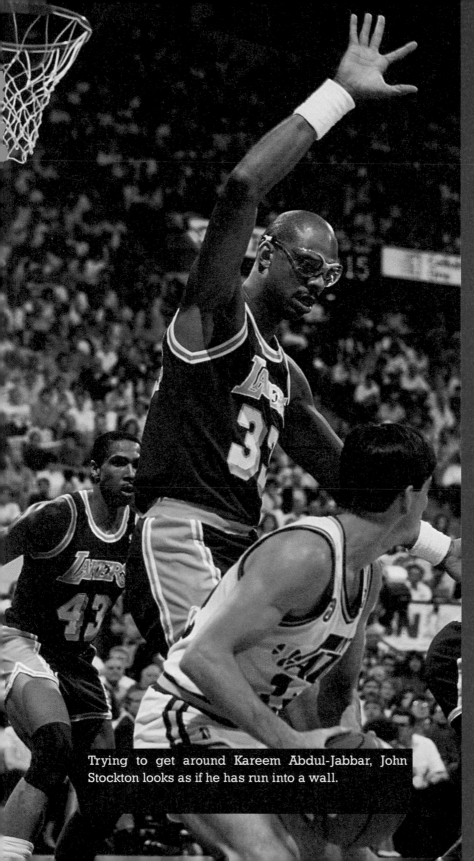

KAREEM ABDUL-JABBAR

Trying to get around Kareem Abdul-Jabbar, John Stockton looks as if he has run into a wall.

Abdul-Jabbar won 4 MVP Awards. He was picked for the NBA All-Defensive first team 5 times.

In 1976, Kareem Abdul-Jabbar enjoyed his best season as a shot-blocker. He blocked 338 shots in 82 games, averaging 4.12 blocks per game. That was the second year in a row that Abdul-Jabbar led the NBA in blocked shots. Still, his shot-blocking success wasn't enough to get his team into the playoffs. The Los Angeles Lakers finished the season 40–42.

"I've often said that an individual's play cannot carry one team or consistently beat another, and the 1975–76 [season] bears me out," Abdul-Jabbar said. "I had the best statistical season of my career, and we missed the playoffs by two games."[3]

In 1978–79, Abdul-Jabbar led the league in blocked shots for the third time. He had 316 blocks in 80 games. One year later, the Lakers acquired Magic Johnson and became the NBA's dominant team of the 1980s. With Johnson helping out with the scoring, rebounding, and assists, Abdul-Jabbar led the NBA in blocked shots for the fourth time in six seasons. He also won his sixth MVP Award. The Lakers won the NBA championship that year. The team went on to win four more NBA titles between 1982 and 1988.

When he retired after the 1989 season, Kareem Abdul-Jabbar was the NBA's all-time leader in blocked shots. That record stood until 1996, when Hakeem Olajuwon took over as the NBA's all-time leader in that department.

After he retired from the NBA, Abdul-Jabbar explained his dedication to excellence by writing, "I think that I've basically played for an idea, which is how close I could come to being at my best."[4]

KAREEM ABDUL-JABBAR

BORN: April 16, 1947, New York, New York.

HIGH SCHOOL: Power Memorial, New York, New York.

COLLEGE: UCLA.

PRO: Milwaukee Bucks, 1969–1975; Los Angeles Lakers, 1975–1989.

RECORDS: NBA record for most points scored, 38,387; NBA career playoff record for most blocks, 476.

HONORS: NBA Rookie of the Year, 1970; NBA MVP, 1971, 1972, 1974, 1976, 1977, 1980; NBA Finals MVP, 1971, 1985; elected to Naismith Memorial Basketball Hall of Fame, 1995; selected to NBA 50th Anniversary All-Time Team, 1996.

Abdul-Jabbar uses his long reach to block a shot from behind, as teammate Magic Johnson gets ready to grab the deflection.

Internet Address

http://www.nba.com/history/abduljabbar_bio.html

MANUTE BOL

Manute Bol pins the ball against the backboard, denying a field-goal attempt.

MANUTE BOL

BEFORE HE BLOCKED HIS FIRST SHOT, Manute Bol tried his first dunk. Bol was in his native Sudan when a cousin talked him into trying to jam it. It must have looked easy, because the skinny teenager was already more than seven feet tall. Bol grasped the ball and eyed the hoop. He ran, leaped, and then broke some teeth when his mouth hit the rim. That may have been when Manute Bol decided that he would be better off blocking shots instead of taking them.

Manute Bol's career stats show that he was always stronger on defense than offense. In every one of his nine NBA seasons, Bol had more blocked shots than points scored. Manute Bol finished with career totals of 2,077 blocked shots and 1,584 points scored.

In the summer of 1982, Fairleigh Dickinson University basketball coach Don Feeley was conducting a clinic for the Sudanese national team. When Feeley saw the nineteen-year-old, seven-foot six-inch Bol towering over all the other players, he immediately asked, "Who's that?"

"That's Manute," the team members answered.

Feeley quickly realized what it meant to have someone seven and a half feet tall protecting the basket. "Boys," Feeley said, "From now on we're going to play a very different game."[1]

Feeley contacted University of Bridgeport coach Bruce Webster. The University of Bridgeport had a strong ESL (English as a Second Language) program, which was ideally suited for Bol. Feeley and Webster were able to get Bol a basketball scholarship to the university.

Manute Bol only played one year of college basketball,

but he still attracted an unusual amount of attention from pro scouts and the national sports media. While playing for Bridgeport, Bol averaged 22.5 points, 13.5 rebounds, and 7 blocked shots a game.[2]

"How good is Manute?" Webster was asked. "Well at this stage if he were playing in the NBA, I think that he'd be the best defensive player in the league."[3]

The death of his father forced Manute Bol to leave college after just one year. He had to go to work to help support his family in Sudan. In the summer of 1985, he began playing for the Rhode Island Gulls in the United States Basketball League.

In his USBL debut, Manute Bol blocked 16 shots. Once again, NBA scouts and coaches were marveling at his shot-blocking skills. Milwaukee coach Don Nelson had played on three NBA championship teams with Celtics legend Bill Russell, and he compared Bol with Russell at his best.

"In 23 years in the game," Nelson said, "he's the most amazing shot-blocker I've ever seen. I imagine that Russell might have done some of the things that Manute can do when he first came in the league, but I never saw him block more than five or six shots in a game. This kid is averaging just under 13 blocked shots a game."[4]

After one short summer season in the USBL, Manute Bol was selected by the Washington Bullets in the second round of the 1985 NBA draft. In his first three preseason games, Bol blocked 18 shots. During the 1985–86 season, Bol became the only rookie in NBA history to lead the league in blocked shots, with 397 in 80 games.

Manute Bol would lead the NBA in blocked shots again in 1989. During his first six seasons in the NBA, Manute Bol was among the league's top five shot-blockers. Bol would also tie the NBA record for most blocked shots in a half (11) and in a quarter (8). Bol left the league after the 1993–94 season.

MANUTE BOL

BORN: October 16, 1962, Gogrial, Sudan.

HIGH SCHOOL: Case Western Reserve English Language School, Cleveland, Ohio.

COLLEGE: University of Bridgeport.

PRO: Washington Bullets, 1985–1988; Golden State Warriors, 1988–1990; Philadelphia 76ers, 1990–1994.

RECORDS: Single-season record for most blocked shots by a rookie, 397; single-season record for most blocks per game by a rookie, 4.97.

HONORS: NBA All-Defensive second team, 1986.

Manute Bol (number ten) was one of the tallest players in NBA history. When his arms were extended, it was almost impossible to shoot over him.

Internet Address

http://www.nba.com/wizards/00400304.html#15

SHAWN BRADLEY

As Mark Jackson of the Indiana Pacers drives through the lane, he can't shake the presence of Dallas center Shawn Bradley.

SHAWN BRADLEY

AT FIRST, SHAWN BRADLEY WAS AN NBA PROSPECT.
Then he became an NBA project. Now he's a full-fledged
NBA defensive star. He was one of the league's top five
shot-blockers from 1993 to 1999.

Shawn Bradley first began getting national attention for
his shot-blocking powers when he was a high school senior.
In the McDonald's High School All-Star Game, Bradley had
6 blocks and altered many other shots. He also grabbed 10
rebounds, scored 12 points, and shared game MVP honors
with Khalid Reeves.

Shawn Bradley's high school coach, Todd Jeffs, credits
Bradley's quickness and long strides as the reasons for his
success as a shot-blocker.

"It doesn't seem like he's moving that fast, but he is,"
Jeffs said. "Two steps of his are like four to a quick guard.
So he'll be under the basket and someone will take what
they believe is an open shot at the three-point line, and he'll
come out and block it."[1]

After high school, Bradley played for Brigham Young
University in Utah. His quickness, agility, and height
(seven-feet six-inches) made him a success. Bradley led the
NCAA Division I players in 1991 by averaging 5.2 blocks
per game. That year, he also tied a Division I record by
blocking 14 shots in one game.

Bradley's college career ended after only one year. The
Church of Jesus Christ of Latter-day Saints (sometimes
called the Mormon Church by outsiders) requires its members to serve as missionaries for two years. When Bradley
was working as a missionary, he had little time for basketball.

Despite his two-year layoff, the Philadelphia 76ers made Bradley their first-round pick in the 1993 NBA draft. Although he averaged 3 blocks per game in his rookie season, he often found himself outmatched by stronger, heavier, and more experienced centers.

The 76ers hired Kareem Abdul-Jabbar to help Bradley work on his game. They also hired bodybuilder Lee Haney. Haney worked at adding weight and muscle to Bradley's body.

In his second year, Bradley's rebounding and shot-blocking numbers improved, but the 76ers weren't satisfied with his progress. In 1995, Philadelphia traded him to the New Jersey Nets as part of a six-player deal.

Bradley didn't let the trade bother him. He concentrated on basketball and finished the 1995–96 season with the best blocked shots per game average of his career (3.65). He also improved his scoring (11.9) and rebounding (8.1) averages.

"I know that I have a long way to go," Bradley said. "But I've always known deep down inside that if I kept working hard and I could get through the tough times, eventually I would make an impact in the league."[2]

About midway through the 1996–97 season, Bradley found that he had been traded again. This time, the Nets sent him to the Dallas Mavericks as part of a nine-player deal. He led the NBA in blocked shots that season, with 248 blocks in 73 games. Shawn Bradley became the first Dallas Mavericks player to lead the NBA in anything.

In 1997–98, Bradley averaged better than three blocks a game for the fourth year in a row. After only his fifth season, Shawn Bradley had 1,171 blocks.

Broadcaster and Hall of Fame player Bill Walton described Shawn Bradley's basketball skills by saying, "He's not a tall guy who happens to play basketball. He is a basketball player who happens to be tall."[3]

SHAWN BRADLEY

BORN: March 22, 1972, Landstuhl, West Germany.

HIGH SCHOOL: Emery County High School, Castle Dale, Utah.

COLLEGE: Brigham Young University.

PRO: Philadelphia 76ers, 1993–1995; New Jersey Nets, 1995–1997; Dallas Mavericks, 1997– .

RECORDS: Shares NCAA Division I record for most blocks in a game, 14.

HONORS: NBA All-Rookie second team, 1994.

Timing his jump perfectly, Shawn Bradley stuffs Rockets forward Joe Stephens.

Internet Address

http://www.nba.com/playerfile/shawn_bradley.html

Mark Eaton

AFTER THE PHOENIX SUNS DRAFTED MARK EATON in the fifth round of the 1979 draft, Eaton didn't sign a pro contract. The seven-foot four-inch center thought that he would be happier turning a wrench than turning away shots.

Mark Eaton had studied to be an automobile mechanic at Cypress Junior College in California. It was only after graduating from UCLA in 1982 that he decided to make basketball his career.

The Utah Jazz made Mark Eaton the seventy-second player chosen when they picked him in the fourth round of the 1982 NBA draft. During his first pro season, many Jazz fans may have thought that Utah should have let Mark Eaton become a mechanic.

Eaton was badly out of shape when he began playing pro basketball. He also tended to get in foul trouble, averaging a foul every six minutes.

But he refused to give up. He was a hard worker and was eager to learn. He spent many hours running, doing drills, lifting weights, and working on improving his game.

About midway through Mark Eaton's rookie season, the Jazz traded center Danny Schayes, and Eaton became a starter. Eaton finished his first year in the pros averaging 3.4 blocks per game while playing only about nineteen minutes a game.

The next year, Mark Eaton became the best shot-blocker in the NBA. He rejected 351 shots in 82 games, for an average of 4.3 blocks per game. That was the first of four seasons when he would lead the NBA in blocked shots.

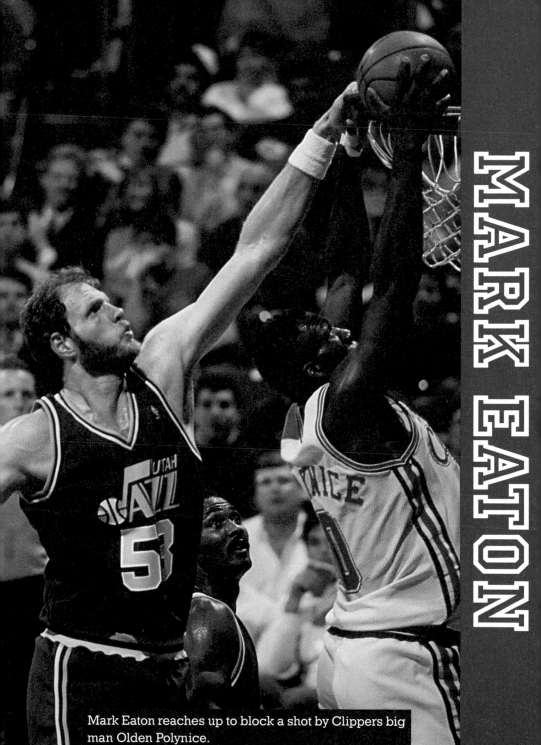

MARK EATON

Mark Eaton reaches up to block a shot by Clippers big man Olden Polynice.

In only his third year in the NBA, Mark Eaton showed everyone how good he could be. Eaton set a record that still stands, by turning away 456 shots in 82 games, for an average of 5.6 per game. That season, there were sixteen NBA teams that had fewer blocked shots than Mark Eaton had by himself.[1] Eaton was also chosen as the NBA Defensive Player of the Year.

Besides stopping two points from being scored, Mark Eaton's blocked shots often added two points for the Jazz. Instead of hitting the ball out of bounds, Eaton would usually tip the ball to a teammate. "Seventy percent of my blocks result in fast breaks," Eaton said.[2] "Even before I make a block, I have a teammate in mind and the direction that I want the ball to go."[3]

Throughout the 1980s, Eaton continued to be one of the most dominating shot-blockers in pro basketball. He led the NBA in blocked shots four times that decade. Eaton was also a two-time winner of the NBA's Defensive Player of the Year Award during this ten-year span. When he retired in 1993, he had 3,064 blocks in 875 games, for a 3.5 average.

"Eaton is a wall," said Kevin Loughery when he coached the Chicago Bulls. "No matter how you try, you don't often get around him. I remember bringing the team into Utah. Mark Eaton just drove Michael Jordan nuts. Michael's got 8 million moves, but Mark intimidated him. Michael couldn't get a shot up."[4]

Mark Eaton knew that he would never be a great scorer or rebounder, so, through hard work and determination, he made himself a great shot-blocker.

"I'll never be the scorer Kareem is, and maybe not the rebounder Moses Malone is, but it's nice to be respected for something," Eaton said. "So people will say, 'Oh, Mark Eaton, yeah he's the shot-blocker.'"[5]

MARK EATON

BORN: January 24, 1957, Westminster, California.

HIGH SCHOOL: Westminster High School, Westminster, California.

COLLEGE: Cypress Junior College, California; UCLA.

PRO: Utah Jazz, 1982–1993.

RECORDS: NBA record for most blocked shots in a season, 456; NBA record for highest blocks per game average in a single season, 5.56; shares NBA playoff record for most blocked shots in a game, 10.

HONORS: NBA Defensive Player of the Year, 1985, 1989; NBA All-Defensive first team, 1985, 1986, 1989.

Mark Eaton had the ability to suffocate players with his swarming style of defense.

Internet Address

http://www.nba.com/jazz/00400490.html#10

Leaping above the rim, Patrick Ewing tries to stop Derek Fisher's lay-up attempt.

THE FIRST TIME Patrick Ewing played basketball, he was the last player chosen. Ewing had recently moved from his native Jamaica to New York City. Shortly after moving to the city, Ewing started watching playground hoops. One day, while he was watching a game, he was asked to play.

Patrick Ewing had never even touched a basketball. He told the boys that he didn't know how to play. They didn't care. "They said it didn't make a difference, they just needed an extra body," Ewing said. "So I played, I started, I messed up. But I liked it, so I kept on playing, kept on getting better."[1]

Patrick Ewing improved enough to lead his high school team to three straight Massachusetts state championships. During the three years that Ewing played at Rindge and Latin School in Cambridge, his team lost only one game. Still, success didn't come easily. Ewing worked very hard at improving his game under the direction of his high school coach, Mike Jarvis.

"He was a hard worker, and if he didn't know something, he'd ask you a thousand times until he got it right," Jarvis said. "He wasn't always a great player. He went through times when he was clumsy and awkward. We had to tell him to be tall, walk tall and be proud of it."[2]

The summer after his junior year in high school, Patrick Ewing had a reason to walk tall and be proud. He had grown to his full height of seven feet, and he became the first high school player to be invited to try out for the United States Olympic Team. He wasn't chosen, but now college coaches all through the United States began recruiting

Patrick Ewing. Ewing, his family, and his coaches listened to many scholarship offers before agreeing on Georgetown University in Washington, D.C.

At Georgetown, Patrick Ewing became a three-time All-American and helped lead the Hoyas to the championship game of the NCAA Tournament three times in four years. The Hoyas won the tournament in 1984. That year, Ewing also played on the United States Olympic Team, which won the gold medal. When he left Georgetown in 1985, Ewing was the school's all-time leading rebounder and shot-blocker.

The New York Knicks made Patrick Ewing the first player chosen in the 1985 NBA Draft. For five straight seasons (1988–92), Patrick Ewing was one of the NBA's top four shot-blockers, and during his first twelve years as a pro, he was always among the top ten in blocked shots.

Ewing's greatest shot-blocking game came during the 1994 NBA championship series between the Knicks and the Houston Rockets. In Game 5, Ewing put the Knicks within one game of winning the title by blocking 8 shots.

After the game, Ewing talked about how his shot-blocking and defensive skills were often overlooked. "People look at my game, they usually look at my scoring, but I do everything else," he said. "Rebounding, blocking up the lane, blocking shots."[3]

Even though the Rockets won the championship series, Patrick Ewing remains determined to play on an NBA championship team someday. Even after becoming the Knicks' all-time leader in blocked shots, scoring, steals, and rebounding, Ewing feels that his career is incomplete without an NBA championship.

"I've won championships at every level except this one," Ewing said. "This is the last one I need to get."[4]

PATRICK EWING

BORN: August 5, 1962, Kingston, Jamaica.

HIGH SCHOOL: Cambridge Rindge and Latin School, Cambridge, Massachusetts.

COLLEGE: Georgetown University.

PRO: New York Knicks, 1985– .

RECORDS: NBA Finals single-series record for most blocked shots, 30; shares NBA Finals single-game record for most blocked shots, 8.

HONORS: NBA Rookie of the Year, 1986; All-NBA first team, 1990; selected to NBA 50th Anniversary All-Time Team, 1996.

Charles Barkley of the Houston Rockets puts up a shot, unaware that Patrick Ewing is ready to swat the ball away from the net.

Internet Address

http://www.nba.com/playerfile/patrick_ewing.html

GEORGE JOHNSON

Flying through the lane, George Johnson looks to make an easy basket.

GEORGE JOHNSON

GEORGE JOHNSON WAS USUALLY A SUB, but he had shot-blocking stats that a starter would envy. In his thirteen-season NBA career, Johnson led the league in blocked shots three times while playing about twenty minutes a game. When the starting center needed a rest or when his team needed more defense, Johnson would come off the bench.

When he graduated from tiny Dillard University in Louisiana, it looked doubtful that the six-foot eleven-inch, two hundred pound center would even have a future in pro basketball. Two hundred pounds is skinny for an athlete that tall. Furthermore, Dillard was not a well-known school, and Johnson had averaged only 12 points a game. One NBA coach joked about Johnson's lack of offense by saying, "Johnson couldn't toss a ball through a hula hoop."[1]

Johnson was passed over for the first few rounds of the 1970 NBA Draft before the Chicago Bulls selected him in the fifth round. Johnson went to the Bulls' training camp, only to be cut from the team.

Johnson was discouraged, but he refused to give up on his NBA dream. He took a job as a supervisor in a bank while continuing to work out and play amateur basketball.

Finally, his hard work paid off. In 1972, the Golden State Warriors gave him a tryout and then signed him to a pro contract. Luckily for Johnson, the Warriors were looking for a certain kind of player to fill a role.

"The Warriors were an ideal situation for me," Johnson said. "They were looking for someone like Nate Thurmond who didn't have to score, but who could play defense, rebound, and set picks for Rick Barry."[2]

During Johnson's rookie season (1972–73), the NBA didn't keep track of blocked shots. In his second year, Johnson averaged just under two blocks per game while playing only twenty minutes a game.

In 1975, Johnson helped the Warriors win the NBA championship by blocking 40 shots in 17 playoff games.

After being traded to the New Jersey Nets in 1977, Johnson became one of the most feared shot-blockers in the NBA. In 1978, he led the NBA in blocked shots, with 274 in 81 games, for an average of 3.38 per game. The next year, Johnson once again averaged over 3 a game, but he finished second in blocks to Kareem Abdul-Jabbar.

In 1979–80, Johnson was again second to Abdul-Jabbar in blocks, before becoming the NBA leader in blocked shots for two consecutive years. The 1980–81 season may have been Johnson's finest year as a shot-blocker. He led the league with 278 in 82 games, for a 3.38 average.

Johnson's shot-blocking numbers declined when his playing time was reduced. Still, in his last season (1985–86), Johnson averaged almost one block per game, even though he was only playing around six minutes a game.

George Johnson is remembered both for his superior shot-blocking skills and as a team player who knew and accepted his role.

"Some players look in the papers in the morning after a game and derive satisfaction from the number of points they score," Johnson said. "I don't. I can't. I have to get my satisfaction from knowing that I maximized my talents, did my best, and contributed something."[3]

GEORGE JOHNSON

BORN: December 18, 1948, Tylertown, Mississippi.

HIGH SCHOOL: J. J. Gulledge High School, Tylertown, Mississippi.

COLLEGE: Dillard University, New Orleans, Louisiana.

PRO: Golden State Warriors, 1972–1976; Buffalo Braves, 1976–1977; New Jersey Nets, 1977–1980, 1984–1985; San Antonio Spurs, 1980–1982; Atlanta Hawks, 1982–1983; Seattle SuperSonics, 1985–1986.

RECORDS: Shares NBA record for most blocked shots in a half, 11.

HONORS: NBA All-Defensive second team, 1981.

George Johnson's shot-blocking ability helped the Golden State Warriors win the 1975 NBA Championship.

Internet Address

http://www.nba.com/spurs/00401098.html#9

DIKEMBE MUTOMBO

His arm fully extended, Dikembe Mutombo knocks the ball out of the sky.

DIKEMBE MUTOMBO

EVEN BEFORE HE BEGAN playing basketball, Dikembe Mutombo loved to stop shots. Mutombo first learned defense by blocking shots as a soccer goalie. He credits his soccer experiences with making him a better basketball player.

"That [playing soccer] helped me with my ability to see the ball coming up and read the angle to react to deflect it," Mutombo said. "I am like a goalie still. I try not to let any of the shots into my net."[1]

After Mutombo finished his college career at Georgetown University, the Denver Nuggets made him the team's first-round pick in the 1991 NBA draft. Mutombo soon showed the Nuggets they had made a wise choice. He was selected to the NBA's All-Rookie team in 1992 after averaging 16.6 points, 12.3 rebounds, and 3.0 blocked shots a game.

In the 1994 NBA playoffs, Dikembe Mutombo's aggressive shot-blocking sent the NBA's most winning team to an early exit. The Nuggets had barely made it into the playoffs, with a 42–40 record. They had to play the Seattle SuperSonics. Seattle had posted the best record in the league, with 63 wins and 19 losses. The Sonics were heavy favorites to beat the Nuggets.

Mutombo inspired the Nuggets by setting a playoff record, with 31 blocks in 5 games. Denver stunned the Sonics by winning the series, three games to two.

"Their game was from the paint, from the inside," Mutombo said. "To me going for blocks was the only way we could win. I kept telling them, 'Don't come!'"[2]

Seattle coach George Karl admitted that Mutombo took the Sonics out of their game. "He got in our players' heads at the very beginning and never left," Karl said.[3]

The Utah Jazz were the next team to face the shot-blocking skills of the mighty Mutombo. It took the heavily favored Jazz seven games to overcome the underdog Nuggets. In those seven games, Mutombo swatted away an additional 38 shots. That series gave Dikembe Mutombo a playoff record 69 blocks in 12 games, for an average of 5.8 blocks per game.

By his seventh season, Dikembe Mutombo had already blocked 2,027 shots. That placed him tenth on the all-time list. One reason Mutombo gave for his success was that he knew when to block a shot.

"If you try to block every shot, you will get into foul trouble," Mutombo said. "You must have good timing and know your opponents, study their shots. You must know when to leave your man because a great shot-blocker is not the one who blocks only on his man. My teammates can take chances on defense, because they know that I'll be there."[4]

After the 1997–98 season, Dikembe Mutombo was named the NBA Defensive Player of the Year for a record third time. He was honored and flattered to receive the award. He made it clear that no matter how many shots he blocked or how many awards he won, there was one more thing left for him to do: "playing in a championship game and winning."[5]

DIKEMBE MUTOMBO

BORN: June 25, 1966, Kinshasa, Congo (Zaire).

HIGH SCHOOL: Institute Boboto, Kinshasa, Congo (Zaire).

COLLEGE: Georgetown University.

PRO: Denver Nuggets, 1991–1996; Atlanta Hawks, 1996– .

RECORDS: NBA career record for highest blocks per game average, 3.7; NBA record for most consecutive years leading the league in blocks per game, 3.

HONORS: NBA Defensive Player of the Year, 1995, 1997, 1998; NBA All-Defensive first team, 1997, 1998; IBM Award winner, 1999.

Robert Pack swoops in for lay-up only to have it rejected by the Hawks' Dikembe Mutombo.

Internet Address

http://www.nba.com/playerfile/dikembe_mutombo.html

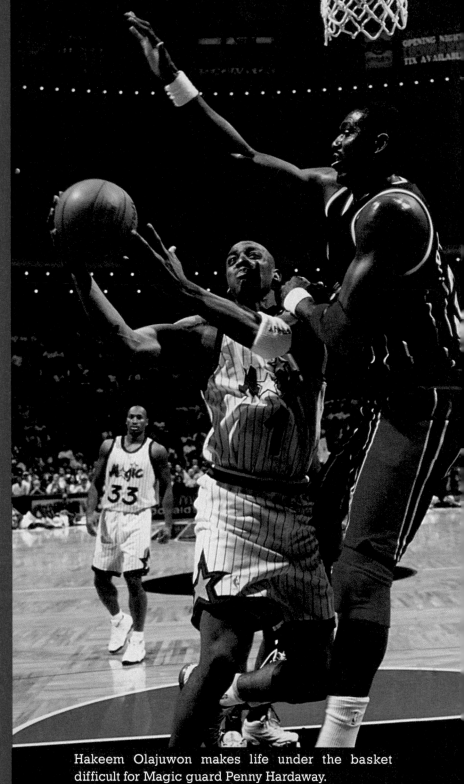

HAKEEM OLAJUWON

Hakeem Olajuwon makes life under the basket difficult for Magic guard Penny Hardaway.

HAKEEM OLAJUWON

WHEN A PLAYER BLOCKS over two hundred shots in a season, he's had an outstanding year. Hakeem Olajuwon did it twelve years in a row (1985–96). In the process, he became the NBA's all-time leader in blocked shots.

In his native African country of Nigeria, Hakeem Olajuwon enjoyed several sports before he played basketball. One day, Oliver Johnson, an American who was coaching the Nigerian national team, gave the athletic teen the incentive to try basketball. Johnson told him, "You learn to play basketball, you can go to America."[1] Olajuwon began practicing with the Nigerian national team, and he quickly became hooked on hoops.

"I did not know any of the rules," Olajuwon said. "Just that this game seemed to combine all of the things I liked from the other games: the footwork, the running, and the jumping. The first day, I blocked shots. I started with that. And then all of the other sports went out of my mind."[2]

Two years after he began playing basketball, Olajuwon got to see the United States as Coach Johnson had predicted. Chris Pond, a United States State Department employee, arranged for Olajuwon to visit some colleges in the United States.

In 1981, University of Houston coach Guy Lewis gave Olajuwon a scholarship. Coach Lewis had Olajuwon sit out a year so he could give him individual attention while teaching him the game's fundamentals.

In 1982, Hakeem Olajuwon was a redshirt freshman. He only played about eighteen minutes a game, but his play helped the Cougars reach the semifinals of the NCAA tournament before they lost to the University of North Carolina Tar Heels.

In his sophomore year, Olajuwon became the starting center for the Cougars. He led the NCAA in blocked shots, and Houston won 25 straight games before being upset by North Carolina State in the championship game of the 1983 NCAA tournament.

By Olajuwon's junior year, Coach Lewis was amazed at how good Olajuwon had become. "I never dreamed that he would be this good," Lewis said. "When he first came here he couldn't make a lay-up. Now he's the greatest shot-blocker I've ever seen."[3] That year, the Cougars once again advanced to the tournament's championship game before losing to the Patrick Ewing-led Georgetown Hoyas.

After the second straight championship loss, Olajuwon entered the NBA draft. The Houston Rockets chose him with the top pick. Olajuwon quickly became what is known as an impact player. As a rookie, he was second in the NBA in blocks, with 220 in 82 games. The Rockets also improved from 29 wins in 1983–84 to 48 in 1984–85.

Still, it took ten seasons before Olajuwon had a supporting cast of teammates who would give the Rockets an NBA title. In 1994, the Rockets won the first of two straight NBA championships. Olajuwon has won both the regular season and NBA Finals MVP Awards. He was also named NBA Defensive Player of the Year. Along with those awards, he has led the NBA in blocked shots three times. He has been selected to the All-NBA first team and NBA All-Defensive first team many times.

Wilt Chamberlain, one of the NBA's all-time great centers and shot-blockers, summed up Olajuwon's hoops skills by saying, "He's in a class by himself. I can't think of another player who's better."[4]

HAKEEM OLAJUWON

BORN: January 21, 1963, Lagos, Nigeria.

HIGH SCHOOL: Muslim Teachers College, Lagos, Nigeria.

COLLEGE: University of Houston.

PRO: Houston Rockets, 1984– .

RECORDS: Career record for most blocked shots, 3,582; shares NBA Finals single-game record for most blocked shots, 8; shares single-game playoff record for most blocked shots, 10.

HONORS: NBA MVP, 1994; NBA Finals MVP, 1994, 1995; NBA Defensive Player of the Year, 1993, 1994; IBM Award, 1993; All-NBA first team, 1987, 1988, 1989, 1993, 1994, 1997; NBA All-Defensive first team, 1987, 1988, 1990, 1993, 1994; selected to NBA 50th Anniversary All-Time Team, 1996.

Hakeem Olajuwon positions himself under the basket, looking to make a defensive play.

Internet Address

http://www.nba.com/playerfile/hakeem_olajuwon.html

DAVID ROBINSON

DAVID ROBINSON'S FIRST BLOCKED SHOT as a pro came against an NBA legend. A crowd of 15,868 fans had come to the HemisFair Arena in San Antonio. They were there to watch Robinson make his NBA debut against the Los Angeles Lakers at the start of the 1989–90 season. Robinson had played well in the preseason, and Spurs fans were eager to see how he would do in a regular-season game.

In the third quarter, the Spurs were up by two when Lakers guard Magic Johnson tried to tie the game by driving hard to the hoop. Johnson attempted a lay-up, which Robinson slapped away. That led to a 6–0 Spurs run, leading to a 106–98 San Antonio victory. After the game, Johnson praised Robinson's performance by saying, "Some rookies are never really rookies. Robinson is one of them."[1]

Robinson's shot-blocking skills first began attracting attention when he was playing basketball for the United States Naval Academy. Oddly enough, when Robinson first entered the Academy, he had little interest in playing basketball. "I didn't care if I played basketball at the academy," Robinson once told a sportswriter. "I just wanted to get good grades and fit in."[2]

Robinson practiced hard and worked constantly at improving his game. During his junior year, he set an NCAA record by averaging 5.91 blocks per game. By the time he graduated, Robinson had set the NCAA records for blocked shots in a game (14), and in a season (207).

As talented as he was, David Robinson was considered a risky pick in the 1987 NBA Draft. After graduating from the Naval Academy, Robinson had to serve two years of

Spurs center David Robinson stops Antonio Davis's attempt at a two-hand slam.

DAVID ROBINSON

active duty in the U.S. Navy before he could play in the NBA. The San Antonio Spurs decided that David Robinson was worth the risk. They made him the team's first-round pick.

In his rookie year, Robinson showed the Spurs that he was worth the wait. He averaged 3.9 blocks per game, to finish second behind Hakeem Olajuwon. David Robinson also made the All-Star team and won the 1990 Rookie of the Year Award. Most important, the Spurs went from a 21–61 record the season before to a 56–26 mark. That was good enough to win the Midwest Division championship.

Robinson did even better in his second season. He earned All-Star and NBA All-Defensive first team honors. He led the league in blocked shots, with 320 in 82 games, for a 3.9 per game average.

Throughout the 1990s, David Robinson continued to be one of the NBA's elite defenders and shot-blockers. He was the NBA Defensive Player of the Year in 1992 and the MVP in 1995. For seven consecutive seasons (1989–90 through 1995–96), David Robinson earned NBA All-Defensive Team honors. During the 1990s, Robinson was among the NBA's top five shot-blockers almost every year.

When they were teammates at San Antonio, Dennis Rodman summed up Robinson's all-around basketball skills by saying, "David's got so much talent it's ridiculous."[3]

DAVID ROBINSON

BORN: August 6, 1965, Key West, Florida.

HIGH SCHOOL: Osbourn Park High School, Manassas, Virginia.

COLLEGE: U.S. Naval Academy.

PRO: San Antonio Spurs, 1989– .

RECORDS: NCAA Division I record for most blocked shots in a season, 207; shares NCAA Division I record for most blocks in a game, 14.

HONORS: NBA Rookie of the Year Award, 1990; NBA Defensive Player of the Year, 1992; NBA MVP, 1995; IBM Award, 1990, 1991, 1994, 1995, 1996; All-NBA first team, 1991, 1992, 1995, 1996; NBA All-Defensive first team, 1991, 1992, 1995, 1996; selected to NBA 50th Anniversary All-Time Team, 1996.

David Robinson gets "all ball" as his block shuts down the Orlando offense.

Internet Address

http://www.nba.com/playerfile/david_robinson.html

TREE ROLLINS

Tree Rollins (number thirty) applies some defensive pressure to his opponent. In 1983, Rollins led the NBA with 4.29 blocks per game.

IT WOULD BE HARD to find a player who blocked more shots while getting less attention than Tree Rollins.

Tree Rollins never played on an NBA championship team or won an MVP Award. Rollins never played in an All-Star Game. He was not someone you would see on a magazine cover or in a shoe commercial. You would just see him if you were driving to the hoop.

Like a tree planted in the paint, Rollins stood in your way. You couldn't go through him. You could only try to get around him. In eighteen NBA seasons, Tree Rollins blocked 2,542 shots and changed the course of many more.

The Atlanta Hawks made Tree Rollins their first-round draft pick after he left Clemson University in 1977. Rollins's rookie year was the first of seven consecutive seasons in which he would be one of the NBA's top three shot-blockers.

The 1982–83 season was Rollins's best season for blocking shots. Rollins rejected 343 shots in 80 games, for a 4.29 per game average. That year he was also named to the NBA All-Defensive second team.

The next season, Rollins earned NBA All-Defensive first team honors while blocking 277 shots in 77 games.

After only nine seasons, Tree Rollins had over two thousand blocked shots. When asked about his success in the NBA, he said that hard work was more important than talent.

"I've never been a talented player," Rollins said. "My success in the league has been from putting in the extra time and doing the extra work I need by studying my guy that I'm playing and concentrating on that one position."[1]

Even as his playing time and shot-blocking numbers

declined, Rollins still took great pride in the way he played. After blocking a shot by Miami Heat rookie Todd Mitchell, Rollins teased the much younger Mitchell by saying, "Didn't you have cable TV growing up young fella? I used to do that all the time."[2]

At the end of the 1993 season, it looked as if Tree Rollins's NBA career was finally over. That year, Rollins had only blocked 15 shots, playing about six minutes a game for the Houston Rockets. Hoping for a coaching career, he became an assistant coach for the Orlando Magic.

Six months later, Coach Rollins became Player/Coach Rollins. Injuries to backup centers Greg Kite and Larry Krystowiak left the Magic without anyone to sub for Shaquille O'Neal. The Magic signed Tree Rollins to a ten-day contract. Rollins played so well that the Magic kept him on the team for the rest of 1994 and for all of 1995.

Magic coach Brian Hill was happy to have Rollins playing again even if it meant losing a valued assistant coach. "He brings us veteran leadership and gives us another seven-footer who can change shots," Hill said. "He knows the game and he's always in the right place at the right time. Not many teams can bring in their backup center and have the same defensive presence."[3]

Even though he was thirty-eight years old, and no longer a starter, Tree Rollins was delighted to be playing and blocking shots again.

"I'm over the hill," Rollins admitted. "I'm old. But I can still be effective for a few minutes. I can go out and play defense and set picks as long as I'm not out there long."[4]

BORN: June 16, 1955, Winter Haven, Florida.

HIGH SCHOOL: Crisp County High School, Cordele, Georgia.

COLLEGE: Clemson University.

PRO: Atlanta Hawks, 1977–1988; Cleveland Cavaliers, 1988–1990; Detroit Pistons, 1990–1991; Houston Rockets, 1991–1993; Orlando Magic, 1993–1995.

HONORS: NBA All-Defensive first team, 1984; NBA All-Defensive second team, 1983.

Tree Rollins moves out to challenge a shot by Hakeem Olajuwon. In 1994, while working for the Orlando Magic as an assistant coach, Rollins was brought out of retirement to play again.

Internet Address

http://www.nba.com/magic/bios/tree_rollins_bio.html

CHAPTER NOTES

Introduction

1. Alexander Wolff, *Basketball: A History of the Game* (New York: Bishop Books, 1997), p. 54.

2. Ibid., p. 56.

Kareem Abdul-Jabbar

1. Elizabeth A. Schick, ed., *Current Biography Yearbook 1997* (New York: H. W. Wilson, 1997), p. 1.

2. Tex Maule, "Lew Turns Small Change to Big Bucks," *Sports Illustrated*, March 9, 1970, p. 25.

3. Kareem Abdul-Jabbar and Peter Knobler, *Giant Steps* (New York: Bantam, 1983), p. 273.

4. Kareem Abdul-Jabbar with Mignon McCarthy, *Kareem* (New York: Random House, 1990), p. 229.

Manute Bol

1. Franz Lidz, "Come See the Dinka, Dunker Do," *Sports Illustrated*, December 10, 1984, p. 74.

2. Maria E. Reico, "Hawking Tall: Marketers Discover Manute Bol," *Business Week*, April 28, 1986, p. 62.

3. John Kavanagh, "Sudanese 7 1/2 Footer Plays in Bridgeport," *The New York Times*, January 20, 1985, sec. 23, p. 1.

4. Bruce Newman, "A Taste of High Society," *Sports Illustrated*, June 24, 1985, p. 54.

Shawn Bradley

1. Bruce Schoenfeld, "Tall Order," *Sport*, December 1993, p. 84.

2. Hank Hersch, "High Hopes," *Sports Illustrated*, March 25, 1996, p. 83.

3. Rick Reilly, "Weight Watcher," *Sports Illustrated*, September 27, 1993, p. 43.

Mark Eaton

1. Jeff Coplon, "How I Do What I Do," *Sport*, February 1986, p. 59.

2. Robert Goldberg, "Clash of the Titans," *Sport*, January 1987, p. 58.

3. Coplon, p. 66.

4. Goldberg, p. 58.

5. Coplon, p. 66.

Patrick Ewing

1. Charles Moritz, ed., *Current Biography Yearbook 1991* (New York: H. W. Wilson, 1991), p. 203.

2. Ibid.

3. Harvey Araton, "Ewing's Magic Trick: Presto! He's Russell," *The New York Times*, June 18, 1994, p. 35.

4. Clifton Brown, "One More Victory Will Mean Parade," *The New York Times*, June 18, 1994, p. 29.

George Johnson

1. Richard O'Connor, "Overachievers," *Sport*, February 1982, p. 38.

2. Ibid.

3. Ibid., p. 39.

Dikembe Mutombo

1. Alexander Bhattacharji, "Dikembe on Blocking Shots in the House of Mutombo," *NBA Inside Stuff*, May 1998, p. 64.

2. Rick Telander, "World Class," *Sports Illustrated*, November 7, 1994, p. 154.

3. Ibid.

4. Bhattacharji, p. 64.

5. "Mutombo Defends His Title," *Tampa Tribune*, May 6, 1998, Sports section, p. 7.

Hakeem Olajuwon

1. Mike Lupica, "The Anti-Shaq," *Esquire*, February 1994, p. 37.

2. Ibid.

3. Bill Gutman, *Hakeem Olajuwon: Superstar Center* (Brookfield, Conn.: Millbrook Press, 1995), p. 22.

4. Lupica, p. 37.

David Robinson

1. Jack McCallum, "He's the Spur of the Moment," *Sports Illustrated*, November 13, 1989, pp. 72–73.

2. Judith Graham, ed., *Current Biography Yearbook 1993* (New York: H. W. Wilson, 1993), p. 498.

3. Jack Clary, *The Best of the NBA* (Stamford, Conn.: Longmeadow Press, 1994) p. 24.

Tree Rollins

1. Tim Turner, "Double Duty Over for Tree," *Orlando Sentinel*, September 30, 1995, p. B3.

2. Zander Hollander, ed., *The Complete Handbook of Pro Basketball*, 16th ed. (New York: New American Library, 1989), pp. 231–232.

3. "No. 1 Backup: Tree Rollins," *Orlando Sentinel*, November 4, 1994, p. G5.

4. Ibid.

INDEX

A
Abdul-Jabbar, Kareem, 6–9, 16, 20, 28

B
Barry, Rick, 27
Bol, Manute, 10–13
Bradley, Shawn, 14–17

C
Chamberlain, Wilt, 5, 36

E
Eaton, Mark, 18–21
Ewing, Patrick, 22–25, 36

F
Feeley, Don, 11

H
Haney, Lee, 16
Hill, Brian, 44

J
Jarvis, Mike, 23
Jeffs, Todd, 15
Johnson, George, 26–29
Johnson, Magic, 6, 8, 38
Johnson, Oliver, 34
Jordan, Michael, 20

K
Karl, George, 32
Kite, Greg, 44
Krystowiak, Larry, 44

L
Lewis, Guy, 34, 36

Loughery, Kevin, 20

M
Malone, Moses, 20
Mikan, George, 4–5
Mitchell, Todd, 44
Mutombo, Dikembe, 30–33

N
Naismith, Dr. James, 4
NBA Finals (1975), 28
NBA Finals (1980), 8
NBA Finals (1994), 24, 36
NBA Finals (1995), 36
Nelson, Don, 12

O
Olajuwon, Hakeem, 8, 34–37, 40
O'Neal, Shaquille, 44

P
Pond, Chris, 34

R
Reeves, Khalid, 15
Robinson, David, 38–41
Rodman, Dennis, 40
Russell, Bill, 4, 12

S
Schayes, Danny, 18
Smith, Elmore, 4

T
Thurmond, Nate, 27

W
Walton, Bill, 16
Webster, Bruce, 11, 12